POVERTY
IS NOT
NATURAL

POVERTY
IS NOT
NATURAL

George Curtis

SHEPHEARD-WALWYN (PUBLISHERS) LTD

First published in 2020 by
Shepheard-Walwyn (Publishers) Ltd
107 Parkway House, Sheen Lane,
London SW14 8LS
www.shepheard-walwyn.co.uk
www.ethicaleconomics.org.uk

British Library Cataloguing in Publication Data
A catalogue record of this book
is available from the British Library

ISBN: 978-0-85683-525-4

Typeset by Alacrity, Chesterfield, Sandford, Somerset
Printed and bound in the United Kingdom
by 4edge Ltd

CONTENTS

ACKNOWLEDGEMENTS

I WOULD LIKE to express my gratitude to my publisher, Anthony Werner, for his careful editing of the manuscript, and to Kai Dattani for attuning it to the concerns of a younger generation.

INTRODUCTION

IN HIS TRAFALGAR SQUARE SPEECH in 2005 Nelson Mandela offered a challenge, which remains relevant to each one of us today, and a call to action:

> Overcoming poverty is not a task of charity, it is an act of justice. Like slavery and apartheid, poverty is not natural. It is man-made and it can be overcome and eradicated by the actions of human beings. Sometimes it falls on a generation to be great. YOU can be that great generation.

The United Nations lists ending 'poverty in all its forms everywhere' as its first Sustainable Development Goal. This is a noble and desirable aspiration, but it is questionable whether the IMF's neo-classical 'trickle down' theory or a redistributive tax system and an expensive, bureaucratic welfare state are adequate for the task. The evidence shows that inequality is on the increase both in the developed and developing world, regardless of economic policy, suggesting the existence of a common cause which neither is addressing.

This book picks up the gauntlet that Mandela threw down and offers a completely different approach, seeking first to establish the fundamental *cause* of poverty worldwide. Drawing on the work of the 19th century American economist, Henry George, whose book, *Progress and Poverty*, probed the question of why it was that, as the Industrial Revolution increased wealth enormously, poverty was not lessened. On the contrary, the richer the society, the greater the inequality. The position remains the same today as it was in the 19th century, again suggesting a common cause, some flaw in the way in which wealth is distributed.

Adam Smith was in no doubt about the cause:

> As soon as land becomes private property, the landlord demands a share of almost all the produce which the labourer can either raise, or collect from it. His rent makes the first deduction from the produce of the labour which is employed upon land.[1]

This raises a moral issue: is it right that ownership of land should entitle the owner to take the lion's share of the wealth produced when they may have contributed little or nothing to its production?

1 Adam Smith, *The Wealth of Nations*, Bk 1, ch 8.

Indeed, if they have contributed, then their entitlement to a share should be based on their labour, just as it would be for their co-workers, not on their ownership of the land.

In fact, is land *ownership* necessary for the efficient functioning of an economy? Clearly, nobody is going to sow if they cannot reap the benefits of their work, so some form of land tenure is necessary to ensure that producers get the product of their labour, but the present economic arrangements have created a system whereby a class of people, landowners, are entitled to a share of the wealth produced without having to contribute to its production, thereby depriving the producers of their full reward. This is a man-made system and is not sacrosanct. It can be replaced by a fairer system.

Henry George expressed a steadfast belief in the efficacy of natural law, properly understood and respected, to erase social problems – problems which, indeed, result from society's denial of natural law. Solving the curse of poverty requires distinguishing what is rightly private property from what is public property, thereby aligning the economy and society with natural law.

This book explores the moral and practical arguments for a major economic reform that would end involuntary poverty by changing the way government is funded. As Nelson Mandela pointed out above: 'poverty is not natural' and 'can be overcome and eradicated by human beings'. He also stressed that 'overcoming poverty is not a task of charity, it is an act of justice'.

1

THE GREAT ENIGMA OF OUR TIMES

'I believe that there is in true Christianity a power to regenerate the world'

Henry George, *The Land Question*

HENRY GEORGE is best known for his 1879 classic, *Progress and Poverty*. This sought to explain why poverty tends to increase and deepen, just as human society becomes more efficient at producing wealth. In his Introduction, he described how 'it was natural to expect, and it was expected, that labor-saving inventions would lighten the toil and improve the condition of the laborer', and how 'the enormous increase in the power of producing wealth would make real poverty a thing of the past'. Yet, in

George's day – and even now in the 21st century – all of these productivity-enhancing forces have failed to abolish widespread 'want and fear of want'.[2]

Observing that poverty is as much a feature where autocratic government prevails as where political power is in the hands of the people, George inferred that there must be a common cause for this failure. He observed that we find the deepest poverty, the sharpest struggle for existence, and the most enforced idleness, where population is densest, wealth greatest, and the machinery of production and exchange most highly developed.

He acknowledged that wealth had been greatly increased by technological progress and the average standard of living had been raised with labour-saving devices making all manner of everyday tasks less toilsome, but in this the poorest did not share.

> I do not mean that the condition of the lowest class has nowhere nor in anything been improved; but that there is nowhere any improvement which can be credited to increased productive power. I mean that the tendency of what we call material progress is in nowise to improve the condition of the lowest class in the essentials of healthy, happy human life.

2 *Progress and Poverty* (1879), Henry George, Robert Schalkenbach Foundation, 1992.

In illustration of this, George offered an image that has been widely quoted:

> The new forces, elevating in their nature though they be, do not act upon the social fabric underneath, as was for a long time hoped and believed,[3] but strike it at a point intermediate between top and bottom. It is as though an immense wedge were being forced, not underneath society, but through society. Those who are above the point of separation are elevated, but those who are below are crushed down.

Unfortunately, Henry George's explanation of the cause of this phenomenon, and the solution he proposed, have received less attention. By and large, history has looked upon Henry George's *Progress and Poverty* more as a stirring call to justice than as a source of rational understanding of social problems, or as a practical means of addressing them. But he warned:

> This association of poverty with progress is the great enigma of our times. It is the central fact from which spring industrial, social and political difficulties that perplex the world, and which statesmanship and philanthropy and education grapple in vain. From it

3 President Kennedy suggested that progress was like 'the tide that lifts all boats'.

comes the clouds that overhang the future of the most progressive and self-reliant nations. It is the riddle which the Sphinx of Fate puts to our civilization and which not to answer is to be destroyed.

Virtually every attempt to solve this riddle has conceived the problem in either/or terms: either society must remorselessly embrace free markets, though under present circumstances many are inevitably left behind, or it must confiscate and redistribute wealth to enforce fairness, though waste and fraud are the inevitable concomitants. Henry George rejected this dichotomy, recognising that under the right conditions labour and capital worked hand in glove.

The problem, George realised, lies with the way economics is taught as he stated in the concluding chapter of *Progress and Poverty*:

> Political Economy has been called the dismal science, and as currently taught, is hopeless and despairing. But this, as we have seen, is solely because she has been degraded and shackled; her truths dislocated; her harmonies ignored; the word she would utter gagged in her mouth, and her protest against wrong turned into an indorsement of injustice. Freed, as I have tried to free her – in her own proper symmetry – Political Economy is radiant with hope.

This remains the case: today's mainstream views on political economy, particularly as they inform public policy, recognize no such 'symmetry'. In George's view, this symmetry revealed that the natural way to fund government was from the rent of land rather than from taxation, and that, in doing so, a major cause of poverty would be removed so that all would share equitably in the wealth produced.

2

JUSTICE IS THE FIRST QUALITY IN THE MORAL HEIRARCHY

'The principles that guide us, in public and in
private, as they are not of our devising, but
moulded into the nature and the essence of
things, will endure with the sun and the moon'

Edmund Burke

HENRY GEORGE saw, just as Mandela did, that it
is only possible to overcome poverty through an act
of justice. In writing 'justice is the highest quality in
the moral hierarchy', he would have been familiar
with St Paul's famous statement '... now abideth,
faith, hope, love, these three: and the greatest of
these is love' (1 Corinthians 13:13). George does not
say that justice is the 'greatest', but that it is the
'highest'. He continued:

That which is above justice must be based on justice, and include justice, And be reached through justice. It is not by accident that in the Hebraic religious development, which through Christianity we have inherited, the declaration "The Lord thy God is a just God" (The essence of Isaiah 45:21) precedes the sweeter revelation of a God of Love. Until the eternal justice is perceived, the eternal love must be hidden. As the individual must be just before he can be truly generous, so must human society be based on justice before it can be based on benevolence.

This, and this alone, is what I contend for − that our social institutions be conformed to justice; to those natural and eternal principles of right ... and this I contend for − that who makes should have; that he who saves should enjoy. I ask on behalf of the poor nothing whatever that properly belongs to the rich. Instead of weakening and confusing the idea of property, I would surround it with stronger sanctions. Instead of lessening the incentive to the production of wealth, I would make it more powerful by making the reward more certain.[4]

If ever a scripture has been bent to the Devil's service, George wrote, it was 'the poor ye have always with you' (Matthew 26:11, also Mark 14:7 and John 12:8). Despite the huge productive capacity of

---

4 *Social Problems* (1883), Robert Schalkenbach Foundation, 1996, p.86.

modern economies, these words continue to soothe the conscience into acceptance of human misery and degradation. Primarily, it bolsters the denial of Christ's teaching, suggesting that an all-wise and merciful Father has decreed that some of his creatures must be poor in order that others should have the good things of life, or in George Orwell's analogy: 'Some pigs are more equal than others.'

George argued that just as man masters material nature by studying its laws, we must discover the great moral laws that govern human relations, and live in accordance with them in order for society to function harmoniously. Thus economic and social policy cannot be framed without careful consideration of natural law. Only in this way can a solution be found for the vice and misery that spring from the inequitable distribution of wealth.

While George believed that 'there is in true Christianity a power to regenerate the world', it must be 'a Christianity that attacks vested wrongs, not that spurious thing that defends them. The religion which allies itself with injustice to preach down the natural aspirations of the masses is worse than atheism.'[5] We can only faintly imagine the

5 *The Land Question*, Henry George (1881), Robert Schalkenbach Foundation, 2009.

wealth-producing powers that would be unleashed in this regenerated social state based on justice, where poverty, and the fear, greed and vice that it causes are banished. What Henry George's political economy suggests is that Christ was not a mere dreamer when he told his disciples that if they first seek the kingdom of God and its righteousness (Matthew 6:33), they could, like the lilies of the field, cease to worry about their material needs. Nor would it be necessary for many to be condemned to monotonous toil.

In his last book, *The Science of Political Economy*, Henry George pointed out that the validity of land ownership had not been questioned by Adam Smith and the classical economists. As economics developed into an academic subject, the status quo was accepted just as slavery had once been accepted. It was only after the publication of *Progress and Poverty* that it had become an issue and that George had discovered that there had been contemporaries of the classical economists who had questioned the validity of landownership.

One such was *The Theory of Human Progression and Natural Probability of a Reign of Justice*, published anonymously in London in 1850. It drew its inspiration from the Bible and the divinity of Christ, arguing that there was a probability of a reign of justice on earth, foretold by scriptural prophecy. Though adhering to the doctrine of the fall of man, the author was an evolutionist, believing that through scientific advances mankind would eventually evolve to a reign of justice and benevolence.

The author, it emerged later, was Patrick Edward Dove, a Scottish landowner and Presbyterian. He argued that the reign of justice would ensure that every human being in the world would at some future time have all their rights restored, and that it is only possible for some to enjoy a privilege at the expense of others. Consequently a reign of justice would ensure the destruction of every privilege and the restitution of every right. He had no hesitation in attacking the vested interests which denied the possibility of this reign of justice, writing:

> Let the political arrangements be what they may. Let there be universal suffrage or any other suffrage, so long as the aristocracy have all the land, and derive the rent of it, the labourer is only a serf, and a serf he will remain until he has uprooted the rights of private landed property. The land is for the nation, and not for the aristocracy.

While George did not share his view that a just solution would arrive inevitably by an evolutionary process, they both recognised that, while universal suffrage gave everyone the right to vote, this of itself did not solve the problem of poverty. What was necessary was for everyone to be able to earn a living and provide for their family, but this was not possible unless everyone had an equal right of access to land – we all need *somewhere* to live and *somewhere* to work. Land is that somewhere and is freely provided by nature to all. It is the concentration of landownership that stands in the way.

Dove argued that just because the State recognises something as private property, this does not give that 'property' moral sanction. He pointed out that the state had often acquired property unjustly or violently. Furthermore, the dignity and authority of the offices of the Church and the power of administering her sacraments, had often been bought and sold.

Nevertheless, though it has long been ignored by societies and governments, and most economists have accepted the status quo, a moral basis for property rights does exist. Down the centuries there have been brave souls who have recognised this and spoken out against the injustice that arises from the private ownership of land, the gift of nature to all. From this truth, Henry George argued, there can be no escape: 'private property in land is a bold, base, enormous wrong, like that of chattel slavery'.[6]

6 *Progress and Poverty* (1879), Robert Schalkenbach Foundation, 1992.

3

LEO TOLSTOY AND HENRY GEORGE

'Slavery has long been abolished. It was abolished in Rome, and in America, and in Russia, but what was abolished was the word not the thing itself'

Leo Tolstoy

AT ABOUT THE SAME TIME as Henry George was writing *Progress and Poverty* in California, Leo Tolstoy in Russia was growing increasingly concerned about the poverty he saw around him. Born into an aristocratic family with big estates, he felt uncomfortable about the large income he received compared with the poor conditions of the peasants. He came to understand that the royalties he received as an author were the fruits of his own labour, while the rent he received as a landowner was the fruit of other men's labours.

When first visiting Moscow in 1881, he was shocked by the beggars on the streets. He did not at first see any connection between their poverty and his own privileged lifestyle, accepting it as an inevitable part of life. Out of compassion he began organising measures of practical relief and charity. When he finally realised that his efforts would never change the status quo, which was supported by Church and State, he began to consider seriously why such poverty existed in the first place.

He observed that while the abolition of serfdom in Russia in 1861 had granted the peasants their freedom, it did not improve their economic condition. Serfs, like slaves in America, were often worse off when freed because as slaves or serfs they were an asset which needed to be looked after. Following abolition they were left to their own devices and many were leaving the country for the towns. Too much of the wealth they produced went in taxes to the State and in rent to the landowner. Tolstoy described this process as 'the passing of the wealth from the producers into the hands of the non-producers'. Henry George saw the very same happening in America, in a country where, though there was no landed aristocracy, the gulf between the rich and the poor was widening as the economy developed.

It is not known when Leo Tolstoy first became aware of Henry George, but the first reference to his work is in *What Then Must We Do?*, published in 1886. There Tolstoy refers to 'Henry George's project for the nationalising of the land'. This, however, was a misrepresentation of Henry George's 'remedy'. By 1892, Tolstoy's reservations had disappeared and once he understood that Henry George was not advocating land nationalisation, he became one of the most outspoken advocates of the tax reform, recognising it as a just and practical way of relieving mankind of the poverty and the social injustice arising out of the private ownership of land. In 1902 he wrote to Tsar Nicholas II, urging this reform:

Dear Brother,

I consider this form of address to be best appropriate because I address you in this letter not so much as a Tsar but as a man – a brother. I did not want to die before telling you what I think of your present activity, of what it could be, of what great good it could bring to millions of people and to yourself, and to what great evil it can bring to those people and to yourself, if it continues in the same direction it is now going.

I think that in our time the private ownership of the land is just as obvious and as crying an injustice as serfdom was 50 years ago. I think that its abolition will place the Russian people on a high level of independence, wellbeing and contentment. I also think this measure will undoubtedly get rid of the socialist and revolutionary irritation which is now flaring up among the workers and which threatens the greatest danger against the people and the government.[7]

The Tsar did not reply – but Tolstoy was persistent. In a long article published in *The Times*[8] in London (Tolstoy's political works were banned in Russia), he argued that merely replacing autocracy with some form of democracy was not the answer. If political reform was the answer, why was there still social unrest, provoked by extremes of wealth and poverty, in the democratic countries of Europe and America? Democratic government may ease the path to reform but does not of itself provide the solution.

Tolstoy came to recognise that there is in fact no need to *own* the land. All that is needed is security of tenure so that one can reap where one has sown, or enjoy the privacy of one's home. It was the

7 Quoted in *Tolstoy: Principles for a New World Order*, David Redfearn, Shepheard-Walwyn, 1992.

8 'A Great Iniquity', *The Times*, 1st August 1905. At the time the Liberal Party in Britain were supportive of Henry George's reform.

absolute ownership of land George challenged, but he had realised how a peaceful reform of land tenure could be introduced through a change in the tax system so that there would be no need for compulsory redistribution. Market forces would do the work. The effect would be to give everyone the same right to use the gifts of nature without acquiring a right of property over nature. So, as Leo Tolstoy came to understand, a right of property can be morally claimed in the house, but not in the land on which it stands.

Henry George's proposal was that, in return for exclusive tenure, each landholder should compensate the rest of society by paying the government a ground rent or, as he called it, a land-value tax. The value of the benefits enjoyed at each site is reflected in the market price of land. The government in collecting the rent to meet public expenditure would be acting not as the monopoly owner of the land, which is land nationalisation, but simply as the agent of society. Once the rent was paid, the landholder would be free to use the land however they wished (within accepted limits of safety and environmental considerations).

4

THE UNFLINCHING SERVICE OF A HOLY ECCLESIASTIC

'Those who make private property of the gift of God pretend in vain to be innocent, for in thus retaining the subsistence of the poor they are the murderers of those who die every day for want of it.'

St Gregory the Great (Pope 590-604)

IN 1881, SHORTLY AFTER the publication of Henry George's *Progress and Poverty* in 1879, Dr Thomas Nulty, Bishop of Meath in Ireland, published a pastoral letter entitled 'Back to the Land', echoing the concerns about private land ownership of both Henry George in California, and Leo Tolstoy in Russia.

Dr Nulty was born in Oldcastle, County Meath in 1816, of farming stock. Apart from his student years at the Catholic seminary and college in Maynooth, his life was spent in agricultural country. Ordained in 1846, he was appointed curate at Trim in his home county. Later he became Parish Priest and Vicar General of the County of Meath. In 1864, he was appointed Bishop of Meath, an office he held for the next 34 years at the Cathedral town of Mullingar. Meath was the largest diocese in Ireland, and contained much fertile and cattle-fattening land. Situated within the Pale, many of its bishops had previously been Anglo-Irish.

Nulty's work in denouncing private land ownership and recognising the moral laws which govern a society coincided not only with Henry George, but also, his Christian faith. For Nulty, the plight of the Irish peasantry under the land tenure system was not only economically unjust, but an infringement of the moral law. He held it as an element of Christian faith that the land is common property and must be treated as such, stating that 'It is essential that the eternal and immutable principles of justice which determine the character of property in land shall in no instance be departed from by the people.'[9]

Nulty was an ardent student of political economy and social science as well as theology. He set before his priests a high intellectual standard and is best remembered for his intense patriotism and labours on behalf of the Irish peasantry. Upon his death, in 1898, *The Nation*, a Dublin newspaper, said of him, 'No prelate of the Church in this country has ever rendered more loyal and unflinching service in the cause of Patriotism, of Right, of Truth, and Justice, than did this holy and learned ecclesiastic'.

Though a passionate opponent of the injustice he witnessed in his diocese, Bishop Nulty was strongly opposed to any form of violence in the effort of rectifying social injustice. This contrasted with the secret society, the Ribbonmen, who some-times resorted to violence in resisting evictions. Nulty was as deeply concerned as they were about the denial of tenants' rights within his diocese, but he wanted to see the introduction of a just land policy without brutality.

Dr Nulty's pastoral letter was addressed to the clergy and laity in his diocese, calling for a radical

9 *Back to the Land*, 1881, Thomas Nulty, Henry George Foundation of Australia pamphlet, 1939.

reform of the Irish land tenure system. He had seen how the system had enabled some landlords to oppress their tenants and how hard-working people of his diocese had been forcefully evicted from lands they and their forebears had tilled for generations to make way for sheep and cattle. The peasants were banished and their homes levelled to the ground. They were left to emigrate or starve, enabling absentee landlords to demand higher rents for their land for cattle grazing. While the population was overwhelmingly Catholic, no Catholic could own land and no Catholic could acquire land by inheritance or purchase.

Dr Nulty's pastoral letter began with the need for legislation to bring about a full and comprehensive measure of justice. Nothing less could satisfy the tenant farmers of Ireland where entire districts of honest, industrious people had been cleared by decadent landlords. However, he had no unfriendly feelings towards individual landlords and he acknowledged that some landlords had been more humane towards their tenants. On the other hand, there was no denying that the land tenure *system* had been frightfully abused by the vast majority of the landlords in Meath.

Looking back over history, Dr Nulty noted that

evil social institutions had long prospered until their true character became generally known. Once seen for what they were, they became unacceptable. Slavery, he pointed out, had existed in every age of the world, not simply as a passing phenomenon, or a temporary result of conquest in war. It had been a long established social and economic institution in unbroken succession, under which thousands upon thousands of human beings had lived and died. Any objection to the degradation in which it held its unhappy victims was dismissed as mere sentimentality. The slaveowner's right of property in slaves was regarded as sacred as that in any other property.

So deeply rooted and so universally accepted was this conviction that the Church itself, Nulty acknowledged, had cautiously abstained from denouncing slavery. It prudently tolerated this crying evil, because it was considered to be simply impossible to remedy. Yet it was the embodiment of one of the most odious injustices. Men, women and children who had not committed any crime or done any wrong to anyone were wantonly robbed of their liberty, bought and sold like cattle in the markets. It was the supreme and most galling injustice that human nature could be called upon to endure.

However, Dr Nulty pointed out, the world's approval cannot justify injustice. The death knell of slavery was only sounded when public attention was fixed on the intrinsic nature of slavery 'by the indignant cry of the great statesman who "denied that man could hold property in man"'.[10] But compensation of twenty million pounds had to be paid to the slave owners for their loss of 'property' to secure the abolition of slavery in the British West Indies. The centuries of practical approval that the world had bestowed upon the institution of slavery had finally failed to justify its continuance.

The system of land tenure in Ireland, Dr Nulty wrote, had enjoyed a long and similarly prosperous career to that of slavery. It could be considered as slavery's twin sister. The vast majority of Irish tenant farmers utterly depended on the arbitrary and irresponsible will of their landlord. Such abject and degrading dependence is, in fact, the definition of slavery.

They toiled in the cultivation of their farms from the beginning to the end of the year, only to witness virtually the whole of the produce of their labour appropriated by others who had not toiled at all.

10 Dr Nulty does not name the 'great statesman', but is perhaps referring to William Wilberforce.

They received even less than the allotted portion given for the maintenance of slaves. They were left with barely enough to keep them alive.

When grazing became more profitable than tillage, hundreds of peasants were evicted from the land to make way for livestock. In an earlier pastoral letter as a priest at Trim, Dr Nulty had recounted the black days when famine had seized hundreds of people, and he described the wholesale eviction he had witnessed in February 1871, where in one day seven hundred people were driven from the homes which they and their forebears had occupied. Many of the families had lived there, tilling the land for generations. Of these tenants, only one owed rent. The people were evicted to make way for cattle and sheep.

The crowbar and the battering ram did their work while armed police stood by. It was the rainy season and, that night, it rained in torrents. At dawn, the people crept out of the ruins where they had spent the night. Where could they go? For miles around, other landlords warned their tenants against giving shelter to any of the evicted. Every man's hand was against them. Those with the means to leave escaped to other lands; many thousands who could not leave passed through hunger and starvation to premature graves.

Dr Nulty concluded by inviting anyone willing to visit his diocese to see the vast and boundless extent to which the fairest land in Europe had been ruthlessly depopulated and abandoned, to become a place of loneliness and solitude more depressing than a desert or wilderness.

At the time of his pastoral letter in 1881, the land question was being hotly debated, both in Ireland and in London. Dr Nulty commented upon the favourable merits of the political debates, urging a return to fundamental principles to solve the problem, stating:

> God was perfectly free in the act by which He created us; but having created us, He bound Himself by that act to provide us with the means necessary for our subsistence ... [E]very individual ... is a creature and child of God, and as all His creatures are equal in His sight, any settlement of the land of a country that would exclude the humblest man in that country from his share of the common inheritance would be not only an injustice and a wrong to that man, but, moreover, it would be an impious resistance to the benevolent intentions of his Creator.[11]

11 *Back to the Land*, p.25.

Given this universal moral imperative, Dr Nulty argued that it was the role of governments to 'bring the largest and most skilled amount of effective labour to bear on the proper cultivation and improvement of the land', and to divide the aggregate produce 'so as to give everyone the fairest and largest share he is entitled to without passing over or excluding anyone'. Nulty acknowledged that because the principle of self-interest is so deeply embedded in our nature, private property in land may seem to be a necessary means of ensuring that people were able to own and keep the products of their labour.

Dr Nulty accepted that, in strict justice, as well as in the interests of the nation at large, a landholder who is constantly improving and increasing the productiveness of their farm has a right to continue in occupation. Thus an improving landholder has by that very fact, in strict justice and in the higher interests of the public, an unquestionable right to continued and undisturbed possession of the land. On the other hand, a non-improving landholder has no right to be left in possession of it. The productiveness of the land is too important to allow this. A nation should not allow a portion of land to remain in the hands of someone who, whether through indolence or incapacity, produces nothing at all, or much less than the land is capable of yielding.

Thus Dr Nulty was quite ready to allow the full benefit of the rights of property in any improvements to anyone, landlord or tenant, who had created them, but pointed out that no landlord or tenant had created the land. If, therefore, any privileged class has a right of property in the land, they alone would have a right to the exclusive use of all the necessities of life. People without this right would therefore have no means by which to support themselves and their families. The well-being, and indeed the very existence of the nation would depend upon the whim and caprice of a single privileged class.

This did not, however, imply that individuals were not entitled to claim payment for improvements to the land. Dr Nulty stressed the point that investments for improvements by industry and labour in land should receive their rightful and just returns. But who, he then asks, has the right to demand a rent for the natural fertility and use of the land, before industry and labour have improved upon its original state? The answer must be the people, the whole community whose collective labour and industry created that value.

Dr Nulty believed that God's gifts were not for sale: He gives and bestows them equally to everyone. No one can have any exceptional right to claim more than a fair share of what was intended equally for all.

> I infer, therefore, no individual or class of individuals can hold the right to private property in the land in a country; that the people of that country, in their public corporate capacity, are and always must be, the real owners of the land of their country – holding an indisputable title to it, in the fact that they have received it as a free gift from its Creator, and as a necessary means for preserving and enjoying the life He has bestowed upon them.[12]

He then distinguishes between individual rights and community rights, stating that usufruct 'is the highest form of property that individuals can hold in land'. On the other hand the cultivator's right of property includes the produce of the land, any improvements he has made and in his undisturbed occupation of the land as long as he continued to improve it. Nulty regarded these rights to be 'founded on the strictest principles of justice'. Their recognition and protection by the State would ensure both national prosperity and social justice.

12 *Back to the Land,* p.33.

He continues by pointing out that there is nothing novel or startling in his reasoning, quoting a number of contemporary eminent economists that support such principles, such as John Stuart Mill's *Principles of Political Economy*:

> The essential principle of property being to assure to all persons what they have produced by their labour and accumulated by their abstinence, this principle cannot apply to what is not the produce of labour, the raw materials of the earth ... When the sacredness of property is talked of, it should always be remembered that any such sacredness does not belong in the same degree to landed property. No man made the land: it is the inheritance of the whole species.[13]

For Dr Nulty, as for Henry George there was

> a charm and a particular beauty in the clearness with which it reveals the wisdom and benevolence of the designs of Providence in the admirable provision He has made for the wants and necessities of that state of social existence of which He is the author. This is a state of social existence in which the very instincts of nature tell us we are to spend our lives.

This provision included 'a great national fund' to meet the expenses of government, a fund which

13 Quoted in *Back to the Land*, p.36.

naturally grows in direct proportion with the growth of the population, which will necessarily occasion greater expenditure. This would cause a virtuous circle, where levied taxation and government expenditure are in harmony with one another. Whereas, where the land of a country is owned by a privileged class, Nulty warned:

> Let the democracy of England and Ireland learn the melancholy fate that has overtaken this splendid inheritance that God has placed in their hands, and which would have saved them millions of sterling which they annually pay by direct and indirect taxation to the government of the country. That patrimony was once theirs by right, and by right it is theirs still; but, in fact, it is theirs no longer: a class has wrested the land from the people of the country and now hold a strict monopoly in it. They sell it out to the people as if it were an ordinary article of private property and solely the result of their own capital and labour. The rents the landlords draw is an income which they derive from the sale of what are avowedly God's gifts, which 'no man made'.[14]

Dr Nulty also condemned the fact that the hardworking people of the nation were being taxed twice: first to benefit the landowners through rent,

14 *Back to the Land* , p.39.

and again to pay millions in taxes to fund government expenditure. Meanwhile, the great, natural fund arising from the rent of land, which Providence had destined to serve as an economic reservoir to cover government expenses, was leaking into the pockets of landowners. Nulty saw how when more development took place upon the land, more wealth would flow to landowners. We see the same today when a new railway can double the value of land through which it travels, causing house prices to soar, due not to improvements made by landowners, but to projects funded by all taxpayers.

Dr Nulty concluded his letter saying:

> Both capitalists and operatives ... are supremely dissatisfied with these disheartening results, and mutually reproach each other with fraud and foul dealing in the division of their common earnings. Their mutual misunderstandings and rival claims to a larger share than they actually receive gives rise to 'lockouts' ... and 'strikes' ... their mutual relations, which ought to be of the friendliest character, have at last settled down into the permanent form of an insane internecine war, which inflicts irreparable injury on the common interests of both. It never occurs to either side that a third party could be liable to blame ... The existing system of Land Tenure, like a great national thief, robs both parties ... of their

earnings for the benefit of a class who do not labour at all.[15]

It is remarkable that Dr Nulty's analysis of economic relationships agreed completely with that of Henry George, despite Nulty having no knowledge of George's work. George remarked in an introduction to an American edition of Dr Nulty's letter, 'It will be evident to anyone who reads this Letter that what is sometimes spoken of as "Georgism" could with quite as much propriety, be styled "Nultyism".'

However, as we shall see in the next chapter, this is unfortunately not the official view of the Church which is a big landowner.

15 *Back to the Land*, p.61.

5

HENRY GEORGE'S OPEN LETTER TO POPE LEO XIII

'Your Holiness, however, is not a servant of
the state, but a servant of God, a guardian
of morals.'

Henry George

TOWARDS THE END of the 19th century there
was growing friction between industrialists and
workers over pay and the appalling conditions under
which so many workers lived and worked. The plight
of the poorest was troubling the conscience of
society, leading many to question whether the socio-
economic system of Europe was morally tolerable,
echoing the same concerns as Henry George, Dr
Nulty and Leo Tolstoy. Such was the fear of
revolutionary change that the Catholic Church felt

it necessary in 1891 to intervene and provide moral guidance in the form of a papal encyclical 'On the Condition of Labour'.

A booklet entitled *Manning, The People's Cardinal*,[16] reveals the build-up of concern in the Church at the time and the influence of Cardinal Manning, Archbishop of Westminster, in its response to the explosive situation developing in Britain and elsewhere. Cardinal Manning was one of the Church's greatest advocates for workers' rights and became one of the most important figures in formulating the Church's response to this conflict between capital and labour. Manning's vision for the Church was clearly demonstrated in his successful mediation in the 1889 dock workers' strike. His negotiations with both workers and employers, to try and build mutual respect for one another to prevent class warfare, were important in bringing the strike to a successful conclusion. His intervention was an example of his vision of Church and people crusading together for social justice, and provided the Church's alternative to Marxism to resolve class conflict. It is probable that if his efforts had failed, violence and class warfare would have ensued. Across Europe, Marxism

16 *Manning: The People's Cardinal*, Don Simpson, 1992.

could have replaced Christian socialism as the basic philosophy of the labour movement.

The following year, Cardinal Gibbons of Baltimore appealed to Manning for help. The growing interest in Henry George's reform and the intensity of support for workers' trade unions in America and Canada was causing alarm in Rome. Gibbons, who had been doing similar work to Manning with immigrants and labourers in Baltimore, had learnt that Henry George's *Progress and Poverty* was about to be put on the Index of Forbidden Books and that an American trade union was to be condemned by the Church. Cardinal Gibbons feared these actions would exacerbate the situation and widen the gulf between the Church and common working people. He appealed to Manning for help. Such was Manning's influence within the Catholic hierarchy and the Pope's confidence in him that no action was taken. Gibbons came to London especially to express his thanks to Cardinal Manning. His intervention had directly influenced the North American Church's social policy.

Manning's sympathy for the poor and reputation as a 'champion' of the working classes had developed from first-hand experience. He had become aware of the plight of the Irish in London and had visited

Ireland to see for himself the appalling suffering of the people who had been evicted to make way for the grazing of cattle and sheep. Their plight had been met with 'colonial' arrogance and indifference from London – he himself had previously scarcely been aware of what was happening. The visit opened his eyes to the injustice suffered by the Irish peasantry, and he called upon the government to reform the land laws so as to end evictions which were driving them to emigrate. When in 1888 the British government appealed to the Pope to dampen Irish radicalism, the Irish appealed to Manning who intervened successfully on their behalf.

The increasingly tense situation throughout Europe led to pleas to Pope Leo XIII to direct the whole Church on social issues, resulting in his encyclical, *Rerum Novarum*, on the condition of labour, published in 1891. Some say it was written by Cardinal Manning. It certainly bears a close resemblance to an address he gave in 1874 at the Mechanics Institute in Leeds on 'The Dignity and Rights of Labour'. Be that as it may, Manning's influence within the Catholic Church and his emphasis on Christian socialism meant that the growing support for George's 'single tax' reform as a remedy for poverty was not adopted by the Church.

In the opening paragraph of his encyclical *Rerum Novarum* the Pope referred to 'the momentous seriousness of the present state of things'. He continued:

> in this Letter the responsibility of the Apostolic office urges us to treat the question expressly and at length, in order that there may be no mistake as to the principles which truth and justice dictate for its settlement.

The encyclical called for a Truce of God to form a new organisation of society based on the concept of equality between capital and labour. It rejected the claims of both laissez-faire capitalism and Marxist socialism and presented an alternative for industrial society. It contended that capital and labour need each other. Workers must not resort to violence or damage property; employers must not exploit workers, but treat them with respect and pay them a 'just standard wage', sufficient for human dignity and care for their moral welfare. However, as part of its 'third way' for industrial society, the encyclical affirmed the right of every person to possess property, in accordance with natural and divine law.

In support of this, the Pope argued that:

It is surely undeniable that, when a man engages in remunerative labour, the very reason and motive of his work is to obtain property, and to hold it as his own private possession. If one man hires out to another his strength or his industry, he does this for the purpose of receiving in return what is necessary for food and living; he thereby expressly proposes to acquire a full and real right, not only to the remuneration, but also to the disposal of that remuneration as he pleases. Thus if he lives sparingly, saves money, and invests his savings, for greater security, in land, the land in such a case is only his wages in another form; and consequently, a working man's little estate thus purchased should be as completely at his disposal as the wages he receives for his labour. But it is precisely in this power of disposal that ownership consists, whether the property be land or movable goods.[17]

A bit further on the Pope expressly states: 'Hence man not only can possess the fruits of the earth, but also the earth itself', arguing that

when man thus spends the energy of his mind and the strength of his body in procuring the fruits of nature, by that act he makes his own that portion of nature's field which he cultivates ... it cannot but be just that

17 *Rerum Novarum*, section 5.

he should possess that portion as his own, and should have a right to keep it without molestation.

Thus the Pope expressly endorsed what Dr Nulty described as 'the twin sister of slavery', using a sophistical argument to distract our attention from the power the large landowner has to evict his tenants by engaging our sympathy for the little man who used his hard-earned savings to buy a small piece of land 'for greater security' (against eviction?). Anyone today, saving for a deposit to get on the 'housing ladder', or having paid off their mortgage after struggling for twenty years or more to meet their monthly payments, can empathise with this. But what if we acknowledge, as Bishop Nulty did, that land is the gift of God to *all* mankind, so that it does not have to be bought? Would not much of that scrimping and saving be unnecessary, enabling people to enjoy a fuller life? However, there must be security of *tenure* so that one can reap where one has sown.

The view expressed in the encyclical has become the established Church position in most of the world, so much so that at the Century Conference in Liverpool in 1991, Norman Willis, General Secretary of the Trades Union Congress (TUC), described how the encyclical had fostered the rapid growth in trade union organisation, particularly in the countries of Western Europe. It was also the inspiration for the formation of the International Labour Organisation, which regulates working conditions throughout the world.

Though *Rerum Novarum* was commonly seen as a response to workers' agitation and growing support for Marxism in Europe, Henry George saw the Pope's justification of private ownership of the earth as an attack on his advocacy of land-value taxation as the means of ending poverty. George responded to the Pope in an open letter, contending that his proposed reform, based on the fundamental teachings of the Christian faith, deserved the Pope's support.

George began by stating his position:

> We hold that this world is the creation of God. The men brought into it for the brief period of their earthly lives are the equal creatures of His bounty, the equal subjects of His provident care.
>
> By his constitution man is beset with physical wants, on the satisfaction of which depend not only the maintenance of his physical life, but also the development of his intellectual and spiritual life.
>
> God made the satisfaction of these wants dependent on man's own exertions, giving him the

power and laying on him the injunction to labor ...

With the need for labor and the power to labor, He has also given man the material for labor. This material is land – man physically being a land animal, who can live only on and from land, and can use other elements, such as air, sunshine and water, only by the use of land.

Being the equal creatures of the Creator, equally entitled under His providence to live their lives and satisfy their needs, men are equally entitled to the use of the land, and any adjustment that denies this equal use of land is morally wrong.

As to the right of ownership we hold that – Being created individuals, with individual wants and powers, men are individually entitled ... to the use of their own powers and the enjoyment of the results.

There thus arises, anterior to human law, and deriving its validity from the Law of God, a right of private ownership in things produced by labor – a right that the possessor may transfer, but of which to deprive him without his will is theft.

George went on:

This right of property, originating in the right of the individual to himself, is the only full and complete right of property. It attaches to things produced by labor, but cannot attach to things created by God.

Thus, if a man take a fish from the ocean, he

acquires a right of property in that fish, which exclusive right he may transfer by sale or gift. But he cannot gain a similar right of property in the ocean, so that he may sell it or give it or forbid others to use it.

Or, if he cultivate grain he acquires a right of property in the grain his labor brings forth. But he cannot obtain a similar right of property in the sun which ripened it or the soil on which it grew. For these things are of the continuing gifts of God to all generations of men, which all may use, but none may claim as his alone.[18]

Clearly these two views are diametrically opposed. The encyclical uses the argument that what is bought with rightful property becomes rightful property. This same argument, that purchase gave ownership, was the common defence of slavery. In language almost identical to the Pope's, it was asked, 'Here is a poor man, who has worked hard, lived sparingly, invested his savings in a few slaves. Would you rob him of the earnings of his toil by liberating these slaves?' In response, George argued:

The error of our people in thinking that what in itself was not rightful property could become rightful

18 *The Condition of Labor* (1891), Robert Schalkenbach Foundation, 2009, pp.210-211.

property by purchase and sale is the same error into which your Holiness falls ... Private property in land, no less than private property in slaves, is a violation of the true rights of property. They are different forms of the same robbery; twin devices by which the perverted ingenuity of man has sought to enable the strong and cunning to escape God's requirement of labor, by forcing it on others.

And when the appropriation of land has gone so far that no free land remains to which the landless may turn, then without further violence the more insidious form of labor robbery involved in private property in land takes the place of chattel slavery, because more economical and convenient. For under it the slave does not have to be caught or held, or to be fed when not needed. He comes of himself, begging the privilege of serving, and when no longer wanted can be discharged. The lash is unnecessary; hunger is as efficacious. [19]

While in Christian countries the cruder form of slavery has been abolished, it still persists at the heart of our civilisation in this more insidious form, explicitly defended in the encyclical by the same fallacious arguments that the apologists for chattel slavery had used in its defence.

---

19 *The Condition of Labor*, pp.231, 232.

Justice could be restored, George explained to the Pope, without disturbing ownership through confiscation or redistribution of land. There is a natural and fair way in which land can be apportioned by requiring the user of land to pay a fee or rent for the privilege of secure tenure and exclusive use. The amount of rent due would be determined by market forces rather than arbitrarily by government. Any improvements such as a house, shop, factory or office, being private property, would not be included in the valuation of the property as they are at present. It is the market value of land alone that would be taxed, hence the name 'land-value tax'. This land-value tax, which is effectively a ground rent, would be paid to the government, not as owner of the land, which would amount to land nationalisation, but as the tax collector on behalf of the nation. If the full market rent were collected, the government would have a secure source of income so that all other taxes could be abolished. This is why it was referred to as the 'single tax'.

George stated that his reform was put forward 'not as a cunning device of human ingenuity, but as a conforming of human regulations to the will of God'. God's commandment not to steal, for example, protected each person's right of property in the fruits of their labour. It follows, therefore, that governments, by taxing what rightfully belongs to the individual, are in breach of the moral law. They create crimes that are not sins (the 'black economy' is a modern example) and punish people for what in itself they have an undoubted right to do. George took the view that it is the moral duty of the state to uphold the distinction between right and wrong and not to weaken the sanctions of religion. Nor must government repress industry, check commerce or punish thrift by taxation, taking by force what rightfully belongs to the producer.

Governments also violate these moral laws when they protect absolute private property in land. This creates a landless class denied an equal opportunity to share in God's bountiful gift to all mankind. Instead of the Christian doctrine of brotherhood, such policies create a society where one person's abundance is secured by restricting the prosperity of others. George insisted that this cannot be God's intended way of providing for everyone.

He pointed out that there is no need for the state to take this unjust course because in the nature of things there is a harmonious way in which, as nations grow and develop, the ground rent would naturally increase with the rising demand for the use of land and thus automatically provide governments with more revenue to meet the greater needs of society. Just as Dr Nulty did, George saw that collecting the land's rental value for public purposes satisfied the moral law, and they recognised in this the benevolence of the Creator.

Government, by not collecting the ground rent to fund public services, is forced to resort to taxation which hampers the creation of wealth, distorts its distribution and corrupts society.[20] It also permits the great inequality in income and wealth that we see in the world today to continue, and ignores the only means by which it is possible, in an advanced civilisation, to combine the security of tenure necessary for improvements with equality of opportunity of earning a living, the most important of all natural rights.

Henry George argued that, though the Pope's recommendations for employers and employees to behave fairly towards each other certainly improved

20 When income tax was introduced in the1830s, J.R. McCulloch, the first professor of political economy at University College London, foresaw the effect: 'Hence it is that the tax would fall with its full weight upon men of integrity, while the millionaire of "easy virtue" would well nigh escape it altogether.' Today there is a sophisticated tax avoidance industry with tax havens.

labour conditions, it was not a cure for poverty, nor was it possible to abolish poverty by the giving of alms – if it were, there would be no poverty in Christendom. 'While the Christian world continues to justify robbery, it is idle to urge charity,' he wrote. It only leads people to think that by giving alms, they deserve to be very well thought of by God. Substituting of vague injunctions of charity for the clear-cut demands of justice opens up an easy means for the professed teachers of the Christian religion of all branches and communions to placate Mammon by persuading themselves that they are serving God.

> Had the English clergy not subordinated the teaching of justice to the teaching of charity ... the Tudor tyranny would never have arisen, and the separation of the church been averted; had the clergy of France never substituted charity for justice, the monstrous iniquities of the ancient regime would never have brought the horrors of the Great Revolution; and in my own country had those who should have preached justice not satisfied themselves with preaching kindness, chattel slavery would never have demanded the holocaust of our civil war.[21]

George concluded his open letter with: 'What is the use of a religion that stands palsied and faltering

21 *The Condition of Labor*, p.297.

in the face of the most momentous problems?' He did, however, express his gratitude to the Pope for the encyclical, saying that it recalled the fact, forgotten by so many, that social evils pressingly concern the Church. He congratulated the Pope for putting a stamp of disapproval on the impious doctrine widely preached, either directly or by implication that the sufferings of the poor are due to the mysterious, unalterable degrees of Providence.

George's appeal fell on deaf ears and today the Church – of all denominations – continues to proclaim a 'social Gospel' under which the faithful are enjoined to work towards a 'just society'. The basic recommendations for doing so are based on the encyclical: the widespread distribution of small, private landownership (a secular version of this is Mrs Thatcher's idea of a property owning democracy) and charity toward the less fortunate. Consequently, within the Christian world and beyond, deep-rooted institutional poverty prevails, private landownership being a primary cause. Neither Pope Leo nor his successors have acknowledged, or refuted, the moral basis of the argument espoused by Henry George, Bishop Nulty and others, so society remains far from the 'just society' called for by the Pope.

6

THE GIVING OF ALMS CANNOT ABOLISH POVERTY

'It is more blessed to give than to receive'

Acts 20:35

CHARITY IS A NATURAL human instinct, encouraged in the West by such statements as the above. The response to natural disasters is astonishingly generous, but feeding the millions living on less than $2 a day is a monumental task which has given rise to a number of large multinational charities, some with NGO status, operating in many countries.

It is of concern to today's Christians, who regard their faith as an upholder of the moral law, that worldwide material progress over the last fifty years has not been reflected in greater brotherhood and harmony among nations, or in the banishment of poverty, despite the generous giving of alms. The task is too big for charity, as Mandela pointed out.

The sheer scale of global poverty was revealed in a letter from the Mother Teresa Children's Foundation, appealing for charitable donations and stating that in Asia, Africa and South America well over 500 million are living in absolute poverty. Malnutrition is the cause of more than half the deaths of children under twelve. Through the Foundation's feeding centres in countries such as India or Malawi, clean water and solid meals are brought each day to starving children and their families. However, every day, the Foundation faces the unbearable situation of having to send starving children away. They say they hope the following day they will have the funds to take them in. They seek to care for children who have no one else to care for them.

Despite the United Kingdom's position as the fifth largest economy in the world, poverty in Britain is by no means unknown. A Christmas appeal from the Salvation Army reminds us that it is easy to forget, among all the glitz of a modern Christmas, that homelessness and hunger are not just stories from the past. Today there are thousands of people who don't have a home, or know where their next meal will come from. The increasing reliance on food banks is evidence of this.

In 2018 the British Red Cross supported nearly 900 refugees arriving in Sicily. The first one to leave the boat was Paulo, just 14 days old. He had spent half of his life at sea, sleeping in a cardboard box. His parents must have been desperate to face the perilous sea in an overcrowded boat in search of safety for their baby. One by one, they stepped from the boat. They looked bewildered, holding up a piece of paper with a number on it, while the authorities took their picture. They had come such a long way with so little.

We often only hear about the Red Cross when they are rushing into areas stricken by disaster. For example, they were first on the ground after the earthquake that devastated Nepal in 2015. However, the Red Cross's work goes beyond the immediate crisis. It has an extensive network of local volunteers in every country, which sows the seeds of long-term change, helping affected communities rebuild their lives and improve their ability to withstand future crises. Immense credit is due to such invaluable aid rendered for many in need.

Likewise Oxfam have shifted from their original focus on famine relief to lifting people out of poverty. They used an ancient Chinese proverb to illustrate the thinking behind this:

> Give a man a fish and you feed him for a day,
> Teach him to fish and you feed him for life.

But this is not the whole story. Once they have learned to fish and are equipped with the tools of their trade, their capital, the fisherman will still have to seek the permission of the landowner to fish on 'his' land. This comes at a price which reduces the income of the fisherman. While skills training may improve the lot of the poor, much of the benefit of the training is captured by the landowner as economic rent.

Henry George pointed out, that so long as the institution of private property in land exists, no increase in productive power can permanently benefit the masses.

> On the contrary, increase in productive power must tend to further depress the condition of those who by progress in the increase of productive power are being crushed down. There is only one way to remove an evil – and that is to remove its cause. Poverty deepens as wealth increases, and wages are forced down as productive power grows, because land, which is the source of all wealth, and the field of all labour, is monopolised. We must make land common

property. Nothing else will do to remove the cause of the evil. In nothing else is there the slightest hope.[22]

The strong bargaining position the landowner has over the distribution of wealth is rarely questioned. Whether this is due to a lack of awareness of the situation or obfuscation to protect vested interests is open to question, but the effect is that the power of the landowner to extract rent goes largely unnoticed today and is a major factor in the increasing inequality of wealth and income revealed in the 2015 Oxfam report.

In his open letter to Pope Leo, Henry George conceded that charity is a noble and beautiful virtue, 'but to commend charity as a substitute for justice, is indeed something akin in essence to those, condemned by your predecessors, that taught that the gospel had superseded the law, and that the love of God exempted men from moral obligations.' He went on:

> All that charity can do where injustice exists is here and there to mollify somewhat the effects of injustice. It cannot cure them. Nor is even what little it can do to mollify the effects of injustice without evil. For what may be called the superimposed, and in this sense,

22 *Progress and Poverty,* Book VI, ch. 2.

secondary virtues, work evil where the fundamental or primary virtues are absent. Thus sobriety is a virtue and diligence is a virtue. But a sober and diligent thief is all the more dangerous. Thus patience is a virtue. But patience under wrong is the condoning of wrong. Thus it is a virtue to seek knowledge and to endeavour to cultivate the mental powers. But the wicked man becomes more capable of evil by reason of his intelligence. Devils we always think of as intelligent.

And thus that pseudo-charity that discards and denies justice works evil. On the one side, it demoralizes its recipients, outraging that human dignity which as you say "God himself treats with reverence", and turning into beggars and paupers men who to become self-supporting, self-respecting citizens need only the restitution of what God has given them. On the other side it acts as an anodyne to the consciences of those who are living on the robbery of their fellows, and fosters that moral delusion and spiritual pride that Christ doubtless had in mind when he said it was easier for the camel to pass through the eye of a needle than for a rich man to enter the Kingdom of Heaven.

It may have the right intentions, and, as valuable and important as charitable endeavours are, they are not adequate to overcoming poverty. Charity cannot supersede justice. The best it can do is ameliorate the effects of injustice.

7

CHRISTIAN SOCIALISM AND THE LABOUR PARTY

'The impetus which drove me first into the Labour movement, and the inspiration which has carried me on in it, has been derived more from the teachings of Jesus of Nazareth than from all other sources combined.'

Keir Hardie

MANY OF THE EARLY LEADERS of the Labour Party were committed Christians. Bob Holman's biography, *Keir Hardie*, published in 2010, provides an insight into the influence of Christianity in the life of a prominent founder-member of the Labour Party. He was born in August 1856 in a one-room house in Legbrannock in Lanarkshire, some ten miles from Glasgow. His mother, Mary Paterson, was a farm servant. In 1859, she married a ship's carpenter, David Hardie, with whom she would have six children. David Hardie accepted Keir as his son, but when he was drunk, he called him a 'bastard'.

Before the Scottish Education Act of 1872 established compulsory education for children, an eight-year old Keir Hardie worked from 7 am to 7 pm. delivering bread and rolls. With David Hardie being out of work, Keir was the only breadwinner, earning three shillings and sixpence a week. Once, after a sleepless night, Keir arrived at the shop fifteen minutes late. Arriving fifteen minutes late once more, on pay-day, on a very wet morning; drenched, barefoot and hungry, he was told to wait 'until the master had finished prayers'. He was then fined his week's pay and told to leave.

After David Hardie returned to the sea, the family moved into the small mining village of Newarthill. Aged ten, Keir worked as a 'trapper' from 6 am to 5.30 pm six days a week, and four hours on Sundays, operating the trap that let air into the mine shaft. At age twelve, he was promoted to draw the pit ponies underground. When the cage that took the men up to the mine surface got 'stuck in the shank', the men below were entombed until the fault was rectified. Waiting at the top, Keir's mother asked why he was not with the men brought up from the pit bottom. He was found sound asleep in the crib with his pit pony.

His mother was keen that Keir should be educated. He may have briefly been given lessons by a clergyman. Despite his limited educational opportunities, Hardie became an able journalist and a miner's trade union organiser. Profoundly moved by the suffering and poverty he witnessed every day. he became an outstanding spokesman in promoting strike action against the working conditions of miners.

To Hardie, Christianity was concerned with the abolition of poverty and immoral working conditions, claiming that those who ignored the social gospel were hypocrites. In 1899, John White, a prominent Liberal chemical manufacturer and a generous supporter of many Christian charities, was raised to the peerage, becoming Baron Overtoun. The hours, wages and working conditions of White's chemical workers were atrocious, leading Hardie to campaign against such conditions and the hypocrisy of his peerage. It was his disillusionment with the Liberal Party that led him to become a founder member of the Independent Labour Party.

Bob Holman reveals how Christianity dominated Keir Hardie's life and that he 'was a socialist whose ideas owed little to Marxism and more to his experience of poverty and his conversion to Christianity'. He saw socialism as the best means of rectifying a society in which some lived in luxury, while others were deprived of the bare necessities of life. However, unlike Karl Marx, Hardie believed such a social system could be achieved by peaceful means, and true to his beliefs, when war broke out in August 1914, then a Labour MP, he opposed Britain's entrance into the First World War, pleading for early peace negotiations. Devastated by the 2,300 soldier casualties on the battlefields every day, he stated, 'Now I understand what Christ suffered at Gethsemane as well as any man living'.

Keir Hardie was in full sympathy with Dr Nulty and Henry George in calling for the establishment of a social system that would eradicate the mal-distribution of wealth. All three believed that such a system should draw its inspiration from the teachings of Jesus, but Hardie regarded socialism as the handmaiden of the Christian religion. As they had this common aim and shared a belief in the power of Christianity to 'regenerate the world', it is pertinent to ask why their approach differed.

Hardie was a trade unionist working in an industrial environment where the employer, the capitalist, set the harsh and dangerous conditions under which labour worked. The power of the landowner to claim a share of the product was not apparent to the workers whose dealings were with their employer. Government intervention was seen by socialists as the means of forcing employers to offer better working conditions.

In the eyes of both Nulty and George, a class war between capitalists and workers need not exist. The key difficulty was that socialists believe that the social evils of a capitalist system stem from a basic conflict between capital and labour. George had witnessed the land-grabbing that was part of the westward expansion of the United States. Thus he could write:

> We have no fear of capital, regarding it as the natural handmaiden of labor, and we look on interest[23] itself as natural and just. We would set no limit to accumulation, or impose any burden on the rich that is not equally placed upon the poor. We see no evil in

23 George was not here talking about 'interest' as the payment for a loan, but in the sense used by the classical economists to distinguish the return to the provider of capital from the return to the providers of land (rent) and labour (wages).

competition, but deem unrestricted[24] competition to be necessary to the industrial and social organisation.[25]

Nulty lived and worked in a rural environment and had witnessed the power of the landowner to clear the land of people in favour of grazing sheep and cattle. He pointed out that, 'The existing system of Land Tenure, like a great national thief, robs both parties [labour and capital] of an enormous amount of their earnings for the benefit of a class who do not labour at all.'[26]

As Nulty also pointed out, the conflict between capitalists and workers arose from a mistaken belief that their interests were at variance, failing to recognise that they were both at the mercy of the landowner. In other circumstances the relations between labour and capital 'ought to be of the friendliest and most cooperative'. George and Nulty recognised land ownership as the root cause of the problem whereas Hardie did not.

Though both Hardie and George saw taxation as the means of achieving their end, the Christian

24 George was not here advocating cut-throat competition but rather competition unrestricted by monopoly and trade tariffs.

25 *The Land Question* (1881), Robert Schalkenbach Foundation, 2009, p.265.

26 *Back to the Land.*

socialist relies on taxing the rich to *redistribute* to the poor, in effect accepting the maldistribution as the natural order and requiring benevolent state intervention to right the wrong. George, on the other hand, saw in the natural order a Divine benevolence which had been disturbed by the human institution of land ownership, and realised that a just distribution of wealth would naturally be restored by taxing land values. There would be no need for *re*distribution.

George considered the very nature of socialism to be in opposition to natural, divine laws because 'socialism inclines towards atheism', and cannot be considered a Christian solution due to its 'failure to see the order and symmetry of natural laws' and hence, 'it fails to recognise God'. However, he acknowledged the value of the work Christian socialists had done to expose the flaws within an economic system that is failing to work harmoniously.

In *Progress and Poverty*, Henry George wrote, 'The idea of socialism is grand and noble, and it is, I am convinced, possible of realisation. But such a state cannot be manufactured. It must grow.' The Welfare State, a product of socialism, has undoubtedly improved working conditions and mitigated poverty, but there are still millions living in poverty in Britain and other industrialised countries, despite the huge cost of social welfare to the taxpayer. An unfortunate side effect has been the creation of a dependency culture.

Christian socialism played an important part in the early years of the Labour Party, and remains a significant factor, but what is less well known is that, as the party grew to become the nation's second biggest political party, a significant number of senior Labour MPs recognised the merit of George's approach. During Ramsay MacDonald's second administration from 1929 to 1931, preparations were made to introduce a land-value tax, George's 'remedy'. The 1931 Budget included provisions for this, but it was never implemented due to the financial crisis of the same year. As a consequence of this crisis, the Labour Party found themselves in a National Government in coalition with the Conservative Party. The land-value tax measures were suspended and later repealed by the Conservatives. The Labour Party thereafter gradually turned to more socialistic remedies.

8

THE INADEQUACY OF SOCIALISTIC REMEDIES

'Institutional charity and political expedients
are no substitute for justice'

Andrew MacLaren MP

IN A SOCIETY rife with poverty and inequality, the motives behind the establishment of a socialist state, offering 'cradle to grave' welfare and state support for vital industries, can be appreciated, and it is understandable why Christians continue to turn towards socialism as the only viable alternative to the ruthlessness of corporate capitalism. This was evident in Cardinal Manning's support of workers' rights in the 19th century, as well as in the recent criticisms of 21st century capitalism by Pope Francis and the Archbishop of Canterbury, Justin Welby.

Pope Leo's encyclical outlined three basic recommendations for improving the conditions of working people. Firstly, the state should step in to prevent excessively long hours of work, to restrict the employment of women and children and to secure in workshops conditions favourable to morals and health. Secondly, it should encourage working men to acquire land. Thirdly, it should allow working-men's associations to be formed.

These remedies, as far as they go, are socialistic. Though the encyclical is not without recognition of the individual character of man and the family, the tendency and spirit of its remedial suggestions lean unmistakably towards socialism, albeit in an extremely moderate form. It is socialism hampered by a supreme respect for private property. George admonished Pope Leo, saying 'you frequently use the ambiguous term "private property" when the context shows you have in mind private property in land'. Leo's encyclical clearly made the point that whatever else may be done, the private ownership of land should be left untouched.

But men do not overwork, George asserted, because they like it; mothers do not send their children to work when they ought to play. It is not the choice of labourers to work under dangerous and unsanitary conditions. All of these troubles come from the sting of poverty – and as long as private property in land continues and some are treated as the owners of the earth and others are charged a fee to live on it, poverty will remain.

The shortcomings of socialistic remedies were clearly observed by one Labour MP, Andrew MacLaren, who had supported the introduction of a land-value tax in Labour's 1931 budget. Having seen these proposals so nearly come to fruition, he became increasingly disillusioned by Labour's change in direction towards an extensive welfare state as a substitute for dealing with the real cause of poverty. He predicted that these welfare programmes would bankrupt the Treasury and only provide short-term relief as opposed to the long-term, self-sustainable cure which was needed. However, he became increasingly isolated in his views and opposed to the Labour leadership so he resigned in March 1943. In his letter of resignation he wrote:

> For a number of years in the House of Commons it has been noticeable that in parliamentary action the Labour Party has attempted to mitigate the results of poverty by compromises and political expedients which did not fundamentally challenge the root

causes of poverty and economic insecurity ... the general line of attack upon social wrong has lacked a clear conception of what these basic causes of poverty are, and what constitutional action should be taken to remove them.[27]

He went on that there was 'a danger that by the promotion of policies which savour more of State reliefs than of direct challenges to these basic social wrongs, the liberty of the individual will be compromised by the growth of State officialdom'. The test of the future, as he saw it, was how best to expand the rights of the community, while also preserving the rights and liberty of the individual. 'To foster one at the expense of the other would lead to disappointment and the emergence of revolutionary movements.' He ended by stating his own position:

> Believing that all men have equal rights to life, which implies the equal rights of all human beings to the enjoyment of those gifts freely provided by nature and necessary to man's existence – land, light, water and air – I hold that it is the first and primary duty of the workers' representatives in Parliament to destroy utterly the private ownership in any of these elements. To allow the basis of wealth production –

27 *Standing for Justice*, John Stewart, Shepheard-Walwyn, 2001.

natural resources – to remain in absolute private ownership means a continual army of unemployed whose presence in the labour market compete with and force down the wages of those in employment; gives rise to speculation around towns, and condemns millions of people to live in slums, checking all health development and necessitating vast health expenditure.

In his open letter to Pope Leo, Henry George pointed out that 'To persist in a wrong, to refuse to undo it', 'is always to become involved in other wrongs. Those who defend private property in land, and thereby deny the first and most important of all human rights, the equal right to the material substratum of life, are compelled to one of two courses.' They must choose either 'the Devil take the hindermost' attitude and deny the equal right to life, invoking the Malthusian doctrine that nature 'brings into the world more than there is provision for', or assert as rights, as socialists do, 'what in themselves are wrongs'. George then quotes an example given by the Pope:

> Denying the equality of right to the material basis of life, and yet conscious that there is a right to live, you assert the right of laborers to employment and their right to receive from their employers a certain indefinite wage. No such rights exist.

Standing as an Independent in the 1945 election, Andrew MacLaren made the point that

> This land of ours would have been the property of the German invaders had it not been for the effort of the common people of this country. Whose land is it now – now we have saved it from the invader? England is God's free gift to the people of England. You are not trespassing on it, although you behave as though you were.[28]

But he was standing in a safe Labour seat and lost his deposit. He must be counted among those who have suffered loss because they resolutely stood on behalf of the truth that Henry George tried to make clear.

28 *The Sentinel,* 3rd July 1945.

9

THE SIGNIFICANCE
OF LAND

'One of the oldest ideas in public finance is
that there are advantages in basing tax on
economic rent'

John Kay and Mervyn King

THE WORD 'LAND' conjures up green fields and
the countryside, but the most valuable land lies
under the buildings in cities. While modern economists still talk of land, labour and capital as the three
factors of production, little attention is paid to land
which is fundamental to all economic activity. As
George reminded Pope Leo, man is 'a land animal,
who can live only on and from land, and can use
other elements, such as air, sunshine and water, only
by the use of land'. *All* wealth is derived from land
by man's work with the aid of capital, be it a spade,

a lathe or a production line. This is a simple fact of life.

It is important to appreciate that land as a factor of production includes not only the dry surface of the earth, but the oceans and seabed, the electro-magnetic spectrum, in short, all that nature provides without human aid. Land is the natural resource from which all human needs are met, but it requires human effort, work, to adapt the provision of nature to meet mankind's daily needs. But not all land is equally productive. This can be due to natural factors like soil fertility or the presence of minerals below the surface, but in a modern economy even more important is location. A simple example will illustrate.

If we take two coffee stalls, one at a central station and the other in the suburbs, the number of coffees sold will be much greater at the central station, so much so that there will probably be three or four stalls to cope with all the customers, whereas at the suburban station there will be slack periods between trains. The difference in the number of coffees sold will not be due to the greater skill or effort of those serving, but to the location. In one case there are lots of customers, in the other few. Whether there are many or few does not depend on the baristas but on *where* they are working. The difference in the productivity is a feature of the location, land, and the measure of that difference is called economic rent to distinguish it from rent paid for the use of a building or equipment.

The classical definition of economic rent was provided by David Ricardo: 'The rent of land is determined by the excess of its product over that which the same application [of labour and capital] can secure from the least productive land in use.'[29] He went on to emphasise the point, stating that it is 'only because land is not unlimited in quantity and uniform in quality, and because, [as population and the economy grow], land of an inferior quality, or less advantageously situated, is called into cultivation, that rent is ever paid for the use of it'. The payment is for the exclusive possession of the site so that the occupier can enjoy the benefits of land of superior quality or more advantageously situated.

The increase in land values as society develops tends to go unnoticed. Instead we refer to 'rising house prices', but this term is misleading. Buildings, being physical products of labour, deteriorate in time, losing their value if they are not maintained.

29 David Ricardo, *The Principles of Political Economy and Taxation*, 1817.

The land on which the buildings stand, on the other hand, does not wear out and appreciates in price with the growth in population and as the economy develops. Talk of 'rising house prices' is really about the increase in the value of land under the buildings. If one compares the 'rebuild value' of one's house insurance with its market value, this will be found on average to be about 50% of the latter – the land does not need to be rebuilt! Capitalised land values represent some 20 to 25 years of economic rent or ground rent.

The criteria used to value land, and thereby the economic rent, will differ for commercial and domestic properties. For the former access to raw materials and market are important – with retail footfall is all-important, so much so that in London's Oxford Street pavements are much wider to cater for the large number of shoppers. For domestic property the main considerations are good transport links, proximity to shopping facilities, good schools and recreational facilities. Quite different criteria apply to the evaluation of buildings: number and size of rooms, state of repair, etc.

Economic rent, or ground rent, is the price a willing buyer is prepared to pay for exclusive use and secure tenure of a particular site. It is a market determined price, not an arbitrary price imposed by government. It measures the value of the advantages the occupier expects to enjoy on the better sites relative to the least productive land in use. It is a surplus or bonus enjoyed by those occupying better sites. Since this surplus is not the result of the skill and effort of the producers, the question arises: to whom then does it belong?

This is a question both the classical economists, like Adam Smith and David Ricardo, side-stepped, as do modern economists. The latter in fact obscure the question further by extending the use of the term economic rent to the return for work and investment. For example, in their chapter on 'Taxing Economic Rent', John Kay and Mervyn King (later Governor of the Bank of England), acknowledge the special nature of economic rent, pointing out that 'most people are familiar with what is meant by rent of land or buildings, but the concept of rent in economics has a specific technical meaning'.[30]

They then go on to define it as 'the amount a factor of production earns over and above that which it could earn in its next best use', and give as an example: 'If a singer earns £100,000 a year, and

30 *The British Tax System,* John Kay and Mervyn King, Oxford University Press, 1990.

his next best employment would be as a barber at £5,000 per year, then he is obtaining economic rent of £95,000'. This ignores the fact that the difference is due to the voice and popularity of the singer and does not depend on *where* he/she sings.

They also mention that 'Gains that arise from the granting of planning permission are treated as capital gains' but the grant of planning permission increases the economic rent, enriching the land-owner not the capitalist. Economic rent applies specifically to the surplus that arises on better land. It is not due to those working on the land or the capital employed, but to the advantages that the land confers on the occupant, so it is a return to land in the same way that wages are the return to labour and interest the return to capital. Those working on the better land cannot claim the surplus as the product of *their* labour or investment. To whom then does the economic rent rightly belong?

Where land is privately owned, as today, the landowner can be entirely absent, and make no contribution to production, and yet still claim the economic rent, as John Stuart Mill pointed out:

> Land is limited in quantity while the demand for it, in a prosperous country, is constantly increasing. The rent, therefore, and the price, which depends on the

rent, progressively rises, not through the exertion or expenditure of the owner, to which we should not object, but by the mere growth of wealth and population. The incomes of landowners are rising while they are sleeping, through the general prosperity produced by the labour and outlay of other people.

In their chapter on 'Taxing Economic Rent' Kay and King refer to Henry George's argument 'that land should be the principal tax base', but they dismiss it on the grounds that the total of economic rents today would be only a small portion of the revenue needed to finance a modern state. This ignores the fact that George proposed *replacing* taxes with collection of the economic rent. The effect would be that, being relieved of other taxes, people would have more money to spend, increasing demand for housing in better locations, thereby increasing the economic rent (and government revenue) for the better sites. At the same time government spending on poverty relief would be greatly reduced. This is why, as Kay and King point out, 'there are advantages in basing tax on economic rent', but this applies specifically to the economic rent of land.

10

A REMEDY FOR
THE 21ST CENTURY

'One of the most important but under-appreciated ideas in economics is the Henry George principle of taxing the economic rent of land, and more generally, natural resources.'

Joseph Stiglitz[31]

IN HIS OPEN LETTER to Pope Leo XIII, Henry George couched his argument in theological terms, appealing to him as a Christian, but the same argument can be made on purely economic and moral grounds, which George did in *Progress and Poverty*. As an economist he sought the 'cause of industrial depressions and the increase of want with the increase of wealth' and offered a 'remedy', which remains as relevant to the problems of poverty and

31 *The Mason Gaffney Reader*, Henry George Institute, 2013.

inequality which still afflict society to this day. He dedicated his book:

> To those who, seeing the vice and misery that spring from the unequal distribution of wealth and privilege, feel the possibility of a higher social state and would strive for its attainment.

Like Nelson Mandela, Henry George was in no doubt that the means of overcoming poverty must first pass the test of being just. He also took the view that such a 'sovereign remedy' must accord with the very nature of things, that 'Liberty is justice and justice is the natural law'. If this is indeed so, then it would not be surprising to find that this remedy would exhibit a wide range of self-reinforcing benefits.

The 'remedy', quite simply, is to change the way in which government is funded by abolishing the taxes which now hamper productive economic activity, and rely on economic rent, the surplus that arises naturally on better sites without the effort or investment of the occupants on those sites, to fund government. In practice this would mean the payment of an annual, market-determined ground rent to the government – not as the owner, which would mean land nationalisation, but as the tax collector on behalf of the nation.

There is little appreciation of how damaging taxes are[32] – in fact they are actually used with the deliberate intent of discouraging certain activity, like smoking. All taxes have this effect, but we assume there is no alternative and have to live with it, though the system has recently been criticised for being convoluted and regressive. Andrew Marr, writing in the *Evening Standard*,[33] denounced a complex tax system which 'punishes honest people'. John O'Connell, CEO of the Taxpayers' Alliance described how the system 'strangles UK enterprise' due to its complexity. With the rise in regressive, indirect taxation since the 1980s and the increased bureaucracy this involves, the system has become far too complex, inefficient and unfair, paying little heed to Adam Smith's cannons of taxation. However, if you are rich enough, you can invest in tax avoidance schemes or place your money in tax havens – one law for the rich and another for the poor.

George's remedy of funding government out of

32 'There is a sense in which all taxes are antagonistic to enterprise – yet we need taxes ... so the question is, which are the least bad taxes? In my opinion, the least bad tax [note the switch to singular] is the property tax on the unimproved value of land, the Henry George argument of many years ago.' Comment made by Milton Friedman during public debate of the American Education League, reported in *Human Events*, 18.11.78.

33 *Evening Standard*, 29th October 2018.

economic rent would level the playing field so that *all* would contribute to the public purse pro rata to the benefits they received from society at large. Those living or working in up-market areas would pay more than those in less attractive areas, or in the country where there are fewer amenities. As we have seen in the previous chapter, economic rent arises as an excess because of the advantages enjoyed by the particular location as compared with the least productive site in use. Currently this benefits the landowner. Collecting economic rent to fund government deprives no one of what they have earned. It is merely taxing the landowner's unearned income, leaving them, and everyone else, free of other taxes, unless 'sin taxes' are specifically imposed to discourage behaviour considered undesirable. This reform would remove a major injustice which leads to the poverty and inequality experienced in the world today. The present situation was aptly described by John Kay:

> You can become wealthy by creating wealth or by appropriating the wealth created by other people. When the appropriation of the wealth is illegal it is called theft or fraud. When it is legal economists call it rent-seeking.[34]

34 *Financial Times*, 27th Dec 2009.

Clearly, 'appropriating the wealth created by other people' leaves the 'other people' worse off, if not impoverished. Landownership confers this power to appropriate the wealth of other people. One example of this power is the demand for payment of a month's rent *in advance* whereas with other transactions the goods are generally handed over first – in most commercial transactions the buyer is given a month's credit before payment is due.

Another aspect of this power, which remains with us to this day, was described by Winston Churchill in an election speech in Edinburgh in 1909 after the House of Lords blocked the Liberal Government's attempt to introduce Henry George's tax reform:

> No matter where you look or what examples you select, you will see every form of enterprise, every step in material progress, is only undertaken after the land monopolist has skimmed the cream for himself, and everywhere today the man or the public body that wishes to put land to its highest use is forced to pay a preliminary fine in land values to the man who is putting it to an inferior one, and in some cases to no use at all. All comes back to land value, and its owner is able to levy a toll upon all other forms of wealth and every form of industry. A portion, in some cases the whole, of every benefit which is laboriously

acquired by the community increases the land value and finds its way automatically into the landlord's pocket. If there is a rise in wages, rents are able to move forward, because the workers can afford to pay a little more. If the opening of a new railway or new tramway, or the institution of improved services, or a lowering of fares, or of a new invention, or any other public convenience affords a benefit to workers in any particular district, it becomes easier for them to live, and therefore the ground landlord is able to charge them more for the privilege of living there.[35]

He ended his speech with these words: 'We do not want to punish the landlord. We want to alter the law.' Henry George's reform is a peaceful means through taxation of ending a privilege that allows some to grow rich at the expense of others. No landholder would be deprived of their right to the exclusive tenure of the land they occupy, but it would no longer be freehold. Instead, they would have to pay a market-determined ground rent to the government but in return they would be relieved of taxation. Their position would be analogous to someone who had booked a seat on a plane who could say: 'This is my seat', but they would not *own* it, nor would they

35 *The People's Rights*, Winston Churchill, Hodder & Stoughton, 1909.

need to. By paying for the ticket they would have secured the right to exclusive use of that seat for a certain period and at an agreed price. Likewise, the landholder could continue to regard it as their land for as long as they liked, subject to paying an annual ground rent, but any buildings or other improvements on the land would be their private property and be untaxed.

Not only would government be funded in an equitable way but, as George argued, with the lifting of taxes which now oppress industry and hamper exchange, the production of wealth would grow rapidly. It 'would be like removing an immense weight from a powerful spring. Imbued with fresh energy, production would spring into new life, and trade would receive a stimulus which would be felt by the remotest arteries.'

This is because there are synergistic advantages to society at large, over and above rewarding the wealth-creators, when wealth is produced. So, for example, having a pub and post office in a village improves the quality of life for everyone in the vicinity. In cities, having local parks and shopping centres with a variety of shops and cafes makes for a more desirable location. The more productive labour and capital are, the greater the common wealth, the economic rent, in which all may share. This synergy is hampered by private property in land, which enables the landowner to siphon off that common wealth. This encourages speculators to hoard land and exclude others from resources which they do not themselves need or use, thereby pushing up the price for others who want to use it. This exclusion and hoarding of land becomes long term and generational. Recent findings show how concentrated landownership is, with just 25,000 landowners owning half of England, with 30% of these being aristocracy and gentry.[36] This deep-rooted issue, the cause of poverty, has evidently existed for generations. When taxes are levied so as to absorb the full economic rent of land, or most of it, land monopolisation would no longer pay. Anyone who wished to hold land out of use would have to pay what it would be worth to someone else who wanted to use it. This would apply to all land, not merely in the countryside. In the heart of the city no one could long afford to keep expensive land from its most profitable use.

Some worry that levying all public revenue from land values would disproportionately burden

36 Guy Shrubsole, *Who Owns England*, 2019.

farmers, who use large acreages to make their living. However, it must be remembered that Henry George proposed a public levy on land *values* – not on acreage. Acres of farmland in the countryside are worth far less than the small plots of land underneath houses and shops etc in the centre of major cities, so ground rent would be highest in towns and cities, where land values are high, and where land speculation now exacts the highest toll. In sparsely settled districts land values are low, so there would be little or no tax to pay. At the same time, farmers would be relieved of employment taxes and taxes such as VAT on improvements. Also, currently, the price of farm land is artificially high because of subsidies. This pushes up the price of land which is bought as a rent-seeking investment, making it more difficult for young people who want to go into farming, rather as buy-to-let investors push up house prices for first-time buyers. The likelihood is that farmers would be better off, could afford more farmhands, be saved a lot of paperwork and would not need subsidies.

The most profound effect of George's reform would be on the labour market. Under present circumstances society is divided into those who own land and those who do not, for example, today's millennial generation who have become defined by their inability to own their own home. Something once considered a cornerstone of generational progress has become a mere dream for much of today's youth. The large landless class have only their labour to sell and, desperate for work to feed, clothe and house themselves and their families, are in a weak bargaining position vis a vis the capitalists and landowners. Competing with each other for employment, the workers drive down wages, often to the point of bare subsistence. It is no coincidence that real wages have been gradually decreasing for over a decade. Labour-saving devices, which enhance production, benefit the employer but reduce the amount of labour required, adding to the competition for jobs and the downward pressure on wages.

Collecting the economic rent from landowners through a land-value tax or ground rent would redress the balance in bargaining power between employer and employee. As it would be costly to hold land out of use or under-use it, the employer would be under pressure to make good use of the land and take on more labour to do so, or let someone else use the land. The increasing demand for labour would drive up wages, and the greater availability of land no longer hoarded by speculators would make self-employment more common – the spectacle of willing workers unable to turn their labour into the things they want would disappear.

The self-employed, this could be as simple as an odd-job man going round doing repairs, would not need to give an account of their income to the taxman; all of it would be theirs to keep. There need be no 'black economy' which is a by-product of income tax and VAT. If they worked from home, their liability would be to pay the economic rent on that property, one payment for both their home and their business, making life much simpler. If they rented premises, they would pay a rent, not the economic rent, to the owner of the building, just as they would if renting a van. The owner of the building would be the person responsible for paying the economic rent on the land under his building, but their business of renting out accommodation would also be tax free.

In fact businesses generally would also benefit from this reform, not only as regards renting premises, but in many other ways. Currently companies are burdened with the administrative cost of the PAYE system and VAT, being effectively unpaid tax collectors for the government. As costs were cut, so businesses would become more competitive internationally.

The beneficiary of this tax reform would not only be labour and capital, but also the government. Population growth and the attendant increased economic activity would naturally push up the demand for land, increasing the economic rent and so government revenue. Instead of enriching landowners, as at present, the government would automatically be in receipt of this rising revenue as the economy prospered. In fact, government could pursue a deliberate policy to increase its own revenue by seeking out ways to provide better services or improved infrastructure, thus giving citizens a better quality of life. As Andrew MacLaren argued back in the 1940s, infrastructure developments could thereby become self-financing rather than saddling the nation with a debt burden.

Another benefit to the government would be the considerable reduction in its collection costs. The complicated network of government bureaucracy involved in collecting the present plethora of separate taxes, each with their own rules and regulations, could be eliminated. The annual ground rent due on each property could be paid in monthly instalments by standing order, saving not only the government but also the taxpayer time and expense. Moreover, it would make tax evasion or avoidance virtually impossible – you can't move your land to a tax haven.

Buying somewhere to live or work would become much cheaper as the purchase price would relate only to the bricks and mortar part of the property, albeit with a liability to take over paying the annual ground rent. This would reduce the size of mortgage required for home ownership or purchasing business premises, reducing the debt level in society and making it easier for one wage-earner to support a family.

Though Henry George labelled his remedy a 'land-value tax', it is not really a tax in that it is not an amount arbitrarily decided upon by government. Instead it would be the market evaluation of the economic rent which society generates on each site. The Valuation Office Agency already separates the value of land from the value of a company's capital when calculating business rate liabilities. Therefore, authorities and bodies already exist that make this crucial distinction. Expanding upon these existing methods used would make the calculation and collection of economic rent efficient and accurate.

In practice this would equate with the annual

ground rent a willing buyer would be prepared to pay to secure the exclusive right to use the site in question. The price would reflect the buyer's estimate of the value of all the external benefits (schools, shops, transport links etc) they expect to enjoy by occupying that location. The government's role would be to keep a public register of all land transactions so as to keep values up to date. Values can go up as well as down depending on changes in the neighbourhood. For example, the closure of a mine or major employer in the vicinity would depress land values,[37] whereas the opening of improved transport links or building of flood defences would increase land values.

George considered that his remedy would achieve the ideal sought by socialists by creating an organic, self-correcting economy as opposed to one constructed and controlled by state regulation.

> Give labour a free field and its full earnings, and for the benefit of the whole community take the fund that the community growth creates to eradicate want and the fear of want. The springs of production

37 The Central Office of Public Interest reported in September 2019 that, as the public becomes more aware of the harmful effects of air pollution, house prices (i.e. the locational value of the houses) could be driven down in pollution hotspots.

would be set free, and the enormous increase of wealth would give the poorest ample comfort. Men would no more worry about finding employment than they would worry about air to breathe. They need no more care about physical necessities than the lilies of the field.[38]

George argued that the reform would also create a different moral climate. Due to the abolition of want, the admiration of riches would diminish and decay, and the respect and approbation of one's fellows would be defined in ways other than the acquisition and display of wealth. Deep-rooted moral and economic issues in contemporary society would be addressed collectively in a way that current policy appears unable to do. The result would be a fairer and at the same time a more economically efficient society, created through addressing the primary cause of injustice.

> We have traced the cause of the unequal distribution of wealth which is the curse and menace of modern civilisation to the institution of private property in land. We have seen as long as this exists no increase in productive power can permanently benefit the masses.[39]

38 *Progress and Poverty,* Book IX, ch. 4.
39 *Progress and Poverty*, Book VI, ch. 2.

The ideas of Henry George are often dismissed as being outmoded or obsolete, the product of a simpler time. Though it cannot be denied that modern economies are more complex than a century ago, it does not change the fact that *all* wealth is produced from land. This is not just the dry surface of the earth, but everything provided by nature, our whole environment. We cannot avail ourselves of the electromagnetic spectrum, for example, without access to land. The masts and cables have to be positioned on land and the landowner can charge for this. The more important difference between George and the present day is that economics is now considered a 'value-free science' to which moral principles are essentially irrelevant.[40] George's belief was exactly the opposite: he argued that society's economic relations are governed by natural, moral laws which society ignores at its peril.

---

40 Surprising confirmation of this was given in a letter to *The Times* on 8th March 2011 from Lord Kalms: 'Sir, Around 1991 I offered the London School of Economics a grant of £1 million to set up a Chair of Business Ethics. John Ashworth, at that time the Director of the LSE, encouraged the idea but he had to write to me to say, regretfully, that the faculty had rejected the offer as it saw no correlation between ethics and economics. Quite.'

11

THE WAY FORWARD

'For man holds in his mortal hands the power to abolish all forms of human poverty ... And yet the same revolutionary beliefs for which our forebears fought are still at issue around the globe–the belief that the rights of man come not from the generosity of the state, but from the hand of God.'

John F. Kennedy

AS NELSON MANDELA pointed out, 'poverty is not natural. It is man-made and it can be overcome and eradicated by the actions of human beings.' What Henry George revealed was the connection between *absolute* private ownership of land and poverty. This widely accepted social institution, just like slavery once was, stands in the way of achieving the first objective of the 17 United Nations

Sustainable Development Goals, ending 'poverty in all its forms everywhere' by 2030. No amount of charity or fine-tuning of the welfare state can overcome poverty so long as land, God's gift to us all, is made the private property of only some. The only effective remedy is to remove the cause.

Henry George realised that the natural distribution of wealth could be restored without any change in the ownership of land through confiscation and redistribution. All that is necessary is for the government, rather than the landowner, to receive the economic rent, making the present complex tax system unnecessary. In return the landowner, like everybody else, would be relieved of the burden of taxation. The corollary would be that all able-bodied people would be able to keep the full product of their labour, their only obligation being to pay the economic rent, the equivalent of an annual ground rent, on any property they occupy. In this context it is important to bear in mind that economic rent is not the product of the occupant's labour. It is a surplus or bonus that arises from working in a more favourable location (see chapter 9), so it is the natural source from which to fund public expenditure and deprives nobody of anything they have personally earned.

Two further benefits would follow. Firstly, no one would want to own and pay the economic rent on more land than they could usefully use, so unused or underused land would be released onto the market for others to use. Secondly, relieving businesses of corporation tax and the cost of collecting PAYE, NIC and VAT would reduce firms' operating costs. This is a very business-friendly reform.

Introducing the reform would not require an increase in the amount of revenue raised. It is not an *additional* tax. It simply means *replacing* the existing complicated system with its plethora of taxes, with the collection of economic rent, hence the term 'the single tax' which is sometimes given to the proposal. Clearly this would have be introduced in stages to allow individuals and businesses to adjust, but the process would be to abolish an existing tax and replace the revenue lost with a percentage of the economic rent of equivalent value, so that the government would not lose any income in the process, and there would be no overall increase in the amount of tax payable. Though the total amount of tax collected would remain the same, individual taxpayers would notice a difference depending on the tax abolished and the value of the property they occupied. A land-value tax is naturally progressive[41] so that the wealthier, occupying more valuable land, would pay more, but the reason they would be paying more is because they would be receiving more benefits from occupying that site – good schools, safe environment, good communications and transport links etc ... They would essentially be paying a market ground rent for the benefits the location afforded.

While currently only a tiny proportion of taxes are actually levied on the economic rent of land, all taxes come ultimately from it, but in a way that distorts the economy. We can test this from our own experience: when we are looking for somewhere to live, we consider how much we can afford. If there were a general reduction in income tax, for example, we could all afford more and competition would bid up 'house' prices, but remember there are two distinct components to 'house' prices: the land and the building. The increase would be in the land component, which is in fixed supply, not the building. The building depreciates over time and has

41 Office for National Statistics data indicate that the top 20% of earners paid about 14% of their disposable income in indirect taxes, of which the main one is VAT whereas the bottom 20%, the lowest earners, paid about 31% of their disposable income in indirect taxes. 2013/14 figures published June 2015

to be maintained at the owner's expense, but it is the landowner who is enriched by the decision of the Chancellor of the Exchequer to cut income tax. The landowner's windfall is not the result of their own efforts, but the result of external events or other people's efforts.

Winston Churchill gave a simple example of this in his election speech, referred to in the previous chapter:

> Some years ago in London there was a toll bar on a bridge across the Thames, and all the working people who lived on the south side of the river had to pay a daily toll of one penny for going and returning from their work. The spectacle of these poor people thus mulcted of so large a proportion of their earnings offended the public conscience, and agitation was set on foot, municipal authorities were roused, and at the cost of the taxpayers, the bridge was freed and the toll removed. All those people who used the bridge were saved sixpence a week, but within a very short time rents on the south side of the river were found to have risen about sixpence a week, or the amount of the toll which had been remitted![42]

42 *The People's Rights*, Winston Churchill, Hodder & Stoughton, 1909.

There had been no improvement in the housing stock, just an added advantage to living in the area, which the market quickly valued at another six pence a week, the ultimate beneficiary being the landowner.

A modern example of this is George Osborne's ' Help to Buy' scheme, the purpose of which is to help first-time buyers get onto the housing ladder – also at the taxpayers' expense. While this has helped many get on the housing ladder (it is more like an escalator than ladder), it has pushed up the price of the land under the buildings, so the ultimate beneficiary is the landowner. Thus, just cutting taxes, as neo-liberal economists tend to favour, enriches the landowner and does not benefit the poor. There is a natural law at work, the Law of Rent which David Ricardo defined (see chapter 9). This works inexorably, just as when you step into a bath you know the water level will rise, so, with people competing for somewhere to live, they drive up the price of land which is in fixed supply. Currently that benefits the landowner not society.

However, this outcome applies only where there is absolute private ownership of land whereby the landowner rather than society gets the economic rent. To the landowner it is simply a windfall so they would lose nothing they had earned if it were taken to defray government expenses. On the contrary they, like everyone else, would be relieved of paying taxes. Henry George's, and Bishop Nulty's, argument was that the government should receive the economic rent. The landowner would be granted secure and exclusive tenure in return for paying an annual ground rent to the government, not as the landowner, but as custodian on behalf of the nation. The amount of ground rent payable would be determined by market forces and would equate to the economic rent. With government in receipt of this revenue, taxes would no longer be needed. Taxpayers being relieved of taxes, would have more money in their pockets, driving up land prices (and government revenue) as more were able to afford a home or place of work of their own, but the requirement to pay a ground rent would discourage land speculation and moderate rises, particularly at the top end of the market.

The objection is often raised about someone living in a large house in an expensive location who cannot not afford an increase in their council tax – often referred to as the asset rich but income poor. Since the annual ground rent would replace the council tax, they could be required to pay the same amount as they are currently paying, with the balance recoverable from their estate in due course. The number of such cases relative to the total number of homeowners is small and could be treated exceptionally as it would only apply for a few years in the transition period from the present complex system.

Another objection raised is of a person who has just taken out a mortgage to buy a freehold property and then finds they also have to pay a ground rent. This ignores the fact that before a land-value tax could be introduced, the pros and cons would have been debated in parliament and the press for several years and, as the likelihood of such a tax being introduced increased, the market would factor this in by reducing prices. Thus anyone buying property close to the time of its implementation would actually pay less for it, thus being an early bene-ficiary of the reform.

Nevertheless this reduction in prices could tip some people into negative equity. This again is a transition problem to be treated exceptionally by, for example, not allowing banks to foreclose so long as mortgage payments were being kept up. Care would need to be taken to avoid adversely affecting banks' balance sheets as a very high proportion of bank lending today is property-related. This poses dangers for the economy as the American sub-prime mortgage scandal illustrated. The careful choice of which taxes to abolish first could ease this problem.

One suggestion put forward in a book entitled *Public Revenue without Taxation*[43] was to abolish employer's national insurance contributions (NIC) and replace the government's loss of income by collecting an equivalent amount of revenue from the economic rent of all business premises. This would fall on the landowner, not the tenant as current business rates do. This would make it expensive for landowners to keep premises empty, encouraging them to reduce their charges to increase occupancy, or sell at a price acceptable to someone who wanted to use the site. It would change the balance of bargaining power between landowner and prospective tenant, and could revitalise the dying high streets by reducing rents. Currently the landowner holds all the aces.

Another important benefit from abolishing the employer's NIC would be to reduce the cost of employment. Currently it costs an employer £27,331

43 *Public Revenue without Taxation*, Ronald Burgess, Shepheard-Walwyn, 1993.

to employ someone on a salary of £25,000. High employment costs encourage employers to out-source jobs to low tax economies or replace people with machines, reducing employment and leaving the government with less revenue to support those who lose their jobs. It would be particularly bene-ficial to labour intensive occupations such as the NHS staff, police, teachers and those working in small, marginal businesses, including farmers, where the reduction in employment costs could make all the difference between survival and failure. The government is the biggest employer in the UK so it would also be the biggest beneficiary.

It might seem unfair to start by relieving the employers rather than the employees of their NIC. The latter would be popular as it would increase take-home pay, but we have seen above how increased spending power pushes up land prices, benefitting landowners without reducing employ-ment costs. It is true that the higher employment levels resulting from reduced employment costs would also increase land prices, but higher employ-ment levels is a public good and the government would benefit by having reduced social security expenditure and increased revenue from a propor-tion of the increased economic rent. This would set in motion a virtuous circle with taxpayers benefiting from the staged reduction in existing taxes and government, rather than landowners, getting an increasing share of the economic rent. Lifting the burden of taxation (economists call it the dead-weight of taxation) would stimulate economic activity and boost GDP.

Another possible starting point could be the abolition of stamp duty accompanied with a reform of council tax to reflect the value of the land only, thereby capturing some of the economic rent for the government. Stamp duty is a transaction tax currently borne by the buyer. As it adds to the cost of moving home, it has the effect of discouraging labour mobility and downsizing. It is true that abolishing stamp duty would also push up land prices just as the abolition of the toll on the bridge across the Thames did, but if the revised council tax captured some of the economic rent, society rather than the landowner would benefit from some of the uplift. If all house owners were required to pay the reformed council tax, regardless of whether the building were occupied or not, it would encourage empty houses to be put on the market, thereby increasing the available housing stock.

While it would be prudent to begin the process

of shifting taxation off economic activity onto economic rent on a revenue neutral basis (ensuring the government received the same amount of revenue from economic rent as it gave up by abolishing a particular tax), removing a harmful tax would stimulate the economy so that the government would soon be receiving more in economic rent than it gave up by abolishing that particular tax. This was pointed out by Joseph Stiglitz, a former World Bank Chief Economist and Nobel Prize winner, who participated with other celebrity economists in a high profile debate on the subject of 'What causes Inequality?' arranged by the Institute for New Economic Thinking in Paris in April 2015. In his concluding remarks he stated:

> ... a tax on land, rents, would actually address some of the underlying problems. This is the idea that Henry George had more than a hundred years ago, but this analysis that I have done, goes one step beyond Henry George. He argued that a land tax was non-distortionary [does not distort economic activity], but this analysis says that a land tax actually improves productivity of the economy because you encourage people to invest in productive capital rather than into rent generating. Well, the result of the shift in the composition of the savings towards

more productive investment leads to a more productive economy, and in the end leads to a more equal society.

While Henry George's 'remedy' would not abolish all poverty – there will always be those impoverished by misfortune, folly or fraud – it would remove a systemic cause of poverty and inequality. In replacing the present complex tax system, which penalises and deters thrift, energy and success, there will no doubt be problems that need special attention but the result would be a society in which all share in its prosperity according to their contribution. What is morally right and natural, would enable the economy to operate with maximum efficiency and ensure that poverty, which is 'man-made', can be 'overcome and eradicated'.

ABOUT THE AUTHOR

GEORGE CURTIS attended seven different village schools in Lincolnshire as his parents moved from farm to farm in search of better paid employment. He started full-time work at the age of 14 in 1939. As a child, Curtis developed a close relationship with all things associated with farming and the countryside.

During his first years in farm employment, farm horses provided the motive power on all farms. It was only during the Second World War that they were replaced by tractors and other farm machinery. As Curtis acquired the skills of his highly skilled fellow workers, he became keenly aware of the poverty-stricken level of wages paid in return for the long hours of dedicated, hard labour. In 1942 he joined the National Union of Agricultural Workers and two years later became a village branch secretary of the union. In the following years he took advantage of the educational opportunities offered by his union as secretary of an active branch.

In 1959 he left farm employment and was

appointed a recruiting officer within Lincolnshire and he eventually became the North Lindsey Union District Organiser, overseeing the union activity of over 100 union branches. He went on to enjoy a long career of over thirty years in this role during which great improvements were made in farm workers' wages and working conditions. He retired in 1990 at the age of 65.

When attending a meeting at the time of his union's objection to Britain's entry into the European Common Market, he was given a book that introduced him to the writings of Henry George. He was then able to obtain copies of all his books and in due course came to recognise that it is the private appropriation of economic rent by landowners, not the claims of the providers of capital, that lies at the root of social ills. It was his reading of *Progress and Poverty* that led him to recognise the potential of the land-value tax, the 'single tax', to eradicate all social ills, inequality and poverty.

During his time as a Labour councillor on the Lindsey and Humberside County Council and member of the North Lincolnshire Council, and as a magistrate, he was frustrated by the party's failure to appreciate that public services could be greatly enhanced if private ownership were restricted to things produced by labour and the economic rent were collected for public revenue.

Ever since his regular attendance at the Louth Centenary Methodist Church in 1945, Curtis has sustained an unshakeable faith in Christianity, and, like Henry George, believes that 'there is in true Christianity a power to regenerate the world'. He became a qualified local Methodist preacher in 1949. His long standing Christian faith conforms with Henry George who said 'his belief may, indeed, be the only ones consistent with a firm and reverent faith in God'.[42]

Following six years of study with the Open University, he was awarded a BSc (Hons) degree in Social Sciences. He felt the study and degree were of little avail because of the complete absence of the philosophy of Henry George from his studies. He believes there is a need to include this philosophy in order for education to eradicate social ills. He believes this also applies to the teaching of the truths that the common people gladly heard from the lips of the Divinely ordained Carpenter of Nazareth.

He owes much during his life to his parents' close association with the countryside, the ever unfailing

42 *The Condition of Labour.*

devotion of his wife during their sixty-four years of marriage until her death in 2011, and the support of his two sons, their wives and families. He is also appreciative of the tolerance of his trade union colleagues over thirty years, and the totally undeserved blessings of Almighty God.

FURTHER READING

Progress and Poverty (1879), Robert Schalkenbach Foundation, 1979.

The Condition of Labor (1891), Robert Schalkenbach Foundation, 2009.

Manning: The People's Cardinal, Don Simpson, 1992.

Keir Hardie, Bob Holman, Lion Books, 2010.

The British Tax System, J.A.Kay and M.A.King, Oxford University Press, 5th ed., 1990.

Public Revenue without Taxation, Ronald Burgess, Shepheard-Walwyn, 1993.

Standing for Justice, John Stewart, Shepheard-Walwyn, 2001.

The State of Freedom and Justice, Michael Horsman, Shepheard-Walwyn, 2016.

From Here to Prosperity, Thomas J. Burgess, Shepheard-Walwyn, 2016.

How Our Economy Really Works, Brian Hodgkinson, Shepheard-Walwyn, 2019.